Hi!
   Well, the last year has been tremendous for me and it is all thanks to you. Your support has taken me to all corners of the globe. I've had many opportunities to meet people and make lots of friends. I've tried to record as much as possible in this annual, so I hope you have as much fun reading it as I had putting it together. Hope you enjoy my movie and the new album and thanks again for your support.
       take care,
              big D,
              Kylie Minogue
                     x

£3.99

CONTENTS:

1988 was a whirlwind year Kylie Minogue will never forget. And 1989? ■ "It's just been fantastic, incredible, so many highlights. I could never have dreamed things would end up like this," a radiant Kylie says. ■ Let's face it, the Melbourne girl who celebrated her 21st birthday on May 28, has every reason to be on top of the world. ■ Kylie is one of the world's most popular and photographed stars. Her singles and albums seem to effortlessly bound to the top of the world's charts, with her acclaimed Neighbours role under her belt her future as an actress is readily acknowledged and still she has retained a charming, bubbling personality. ■ When trying to analyse Kylie's fame, one of the questions she most frequently gets asked is, why you? ■ "Yes, it's true," she laughs. "Everybody asks that. The best explanation I can come up with is that you have to have some talent and you also have to have a bit of luck. I also think it's normality, just being a normal person, people can relate to me. I think a lot of people think 'Gee, that could be me. She's pretty normal, so that could be me one day'." ■ This past year Kylie has again been on a gruelling schedule working almost non-stop, but the rewards have been some of the most successful and enjoyable times of her career. ■ Winding back the clock to late last year, Neighbours euphoria meant Kylie was in constant demand for interviews and appearances. The series continually peaked in Britain's top three shows, with up to 20 million viewers. It seemed everyone was talking about Neighbours — particularly Scott and Charlene's relationship. ■ True love won out and the couple's on screen wedding earlier this year received enormous viewing figures and had everyone off to the local record shop to buy the theme song *Suddenly* by Angry Anderson.

In November 1988 the Neighbours cast flew from Australia to be special guests at the Royal Variety Performance before Princess Margaret and one of the show's biggest fans, the Queen Mother. ■ Kylie had in fact said a sad farewell to the series six months earlier, although she continues to be on screen in Britain because of the backlog of episodes. ■ After performing *I Should Be So Lucky* and a new song *Made In Heaven,* Kylie introduced the cast who acted a sketch about being neighbourly and sang the theme song. ■ "Appearing was a great thrill," Kylie told the media at the time. "It has topped off a wonderful year." ■ Little did she know the year still held a few surprises. The very next week the eagerly awaited duet with Jason Donovan *Especially For You* was released to massive pre-order sales. Book-makers were confident it would claim the Christmas number one spot, but it was not to be.

■ Cliff Richard's *Mistletoe and Wine* clung to the top spot with the duet reaching number two. Still Kylie ended the year with the biggest selling UK album of 1988, the number one longplay video and the number two single. Not bad! ■ With Christmas festivities barely over, Kylie was off for promotional work in America, where *The Locomotion* had reached number three. In Australia her manager, Terry Blamey, made a major announcement to the press. ■ After sifting through dozens of film scripts and mini-series offers, Kylie had signed to star in a feature film called *The Delinquents*. Media interest was heightened when it was revealed David Bowie would be the film's co-producer and co-ordinator of the soundtrack. ■ The $8.5 million film is set in Australia in the 1950s and is based on the book of the same title written in 1962 by the late Criena Rohan. Ms Rohan's real name was in fact Criena Cash, aunt of Aussie tennis player Pat Cash!

Kylie plays Lola Lovell, a young woman living with her mother who works in a pub in the Northern Australian town of Bundaberg. Her love affair with Brownie is frowned upon by the residents of the town, forcing the young lovers to flee, travelling to Sydney and Melbourne. ■ What was it about this particular film that so excited Kylie and lured her back to acting? ■ "Firstly, I really enjoyed the story. It is a very mature love story, not puppy love stuff. The society of the time was really against them so there is a lot of strength in their characters to keep going. ■ "Lola is very different to Charlene too and I felt that was important. And being set in the '50s, I mean I love the whole '50s scene, the fashion, the music, all that, so the idea of it being set then was very appealing." ■ Filming took place in Queensland in May and June, an experience Kylie found professionally of great benefit and personally great fun. ■ "It reminded me a bit of my Neighbours days, having a cast and crew who became just like a big family. You're spending every day week in week out with the same people, so you end up becoming really good friends," she says. ■ Knowing the critics of the world would be expectantly awaiting her first movie role, Kylie admits to having been quite nervous, but she couldn't be happier with the final result. ■ "There are so many things I learnt because we did work extremely hard, but we had a wonderful time as well. I'm really pleased with it. I just hope everybody else likes it too." ■ *The Delinquents* will be released in Britain and Australia around Christmas, accompanied by the David Bowie produced soundtrack. ■ While Kylie was locked away in Queensland filming, a new single, *Hand On Your Heart,* had rocketed up the British charts. The song had been recorded in London in February again with Stock, Aitken and Waterman at the helm. Released in April with another lively and entertaining video to support it, the single continued Kylie's amazing run of hits.

with my dancers, Richard, Martin, Venol & Kevin, living in Paris.

They found measurements I never knew I had. Mmm... nostril to nostril — very handy!!

my hotel — no Universal Studios

Just hangin' with my manager Terry at the London Docklands.

They wanted to put me in the 'Chamber of Horrors' at Madame Tussaud's.

N-n-n-never bbb-been so c-c-cc-c COLD. Jen and I on a tourist boat going down the River Seine. Bbrrr!

Jennifer and myself grooving at about 39,000 ft above!!

Such was her popularity in Britain, Kylie became the recipient of two most famous tributes. Madame Tussaud's waxworks invited her for a three-hour sitting to make a cast of her face, and in April the completed "dummy" joins the likes of The Beatles, Michael Jackson and David Bowie on display. ■ Next, Kylie really knew she'd made it when she became the latest victim of the notorious Spitting Image TV programme. The show modelled a puppet on her to join the Royals, politicians and famous stars — a sure sign she had become a household name. ■ On a more serious note, Kylie's next major project was the recording of album number two. Almost without a break following *The Delinquents,* she flew to London for an intensive period of studio work. ■ The pressure to match the success of the Kylie album was enormous but with more experience and confidence than ever before, she was determined to make a higher quality and more entertaining record. ■ Released in September, the next few months will determine if Kylie's hopes about the album are realised. ■ The success that Kylie, or for that matter any star, achieves unfortunately comes at a price. For Kylie it has been a tiring schedule of international travel and commitments, leaving little time to simply relax or pursue other activities. ■ The frustration arising from a loss of privacy, of always being recognised and approached, is difficult to overcome, and then there's the media. ■ Always hungry for stories to sell their newspapers, all sorts of wild tales are made up, no matter how cruel or unkind. This year Kylie has been labelled an anorexic, a sulk, a bitch and even an alien! And that's just to name a few. ■ For someone under the harsh glare of the media spotlight for so long, Kylie has handled herself with remarkable dignity and control. ■ Still, she admits: "There have been times when it has got to me. I have gone home and cried. I'm human. I'm not made of steel. But it is usually over-tiredness."

"It was hard at first because I thought 'What have I done? I haven't done anything'. All I've tried to do is to make people happy and bring enjoyment. I thought 'What did I do to deserve this?'. I didn't think it was fair. ■ "But I've come to realise it happens to everyone and the bigger you get the more it will happen. I have definitely become more resistant to the media and the pressure. ■ "I'm tougher now. If I wasn't, I would have fizzled away by now." ■ Asked if she would change anything if she had her time over again Kylie says: "There's a lot in my teenage years, but we probably all say that. The main thing is that I would like to slow things down. A few more years and a few less things to do." ■ And if she hadn't pursued a show business career, what would she be doing now? ■ "I would always do something creative. If my singing and acting career ended I would probably get involved in graphic design or fashion. I was thinking of becoming a fashion designer at one stage because I'm very resourceful when it comes to clothes. ■ "I have a large box of fabric off-cuts waiting for me to do something with. ■ "I've also always had a secret ambition to run a shop, a sort of gift shop full of knick knacks. I like to make a lot of crafty things at home, so I could see myself doing that for sure." ■ Some papers would have us believe Kylie is a multi-millionairess with a lavish lifestyle, but nothing could be further from the truth. ■ To safeguard her future Kylie has bought a house in Melbourne as an investment, but she still prefers to live at home with the family and dog Gabby. ■ And that seems a perfect place to leave Kylie for now. What a remarkable year it's been. Roll on 1990!

WILD RUMOURS AND SILLY NEWSPAPER STORIES— KYLIE'S LIFE IS FULL OF 'EM!

There's no doubt Kylie has been one of the most talked about and photographed stars of the year. ■ But with all the front pages, magazine covers, articles and pin-ups there is the other side. Success brings with it some pretty wild rumours, most of them so ridiculously untrue Kylie just has to laugh. ■ Here's some of the best "stories":

◀ Kylie's big hit *I Should Be So Lucky* was sung by Rick Astley and slowed down!

◀ Kylie had an affair with Blue Mercedes singer David Titlowe, who she's never even met.

◀ She was offered one million dollars to pose nude for a "raunchy" girlie magazine. Kylie was apparently told by the magazine "Why not go the whole hog and make yourself a small fortune?" to which she was reported as answering "My Mum and Dad would go absolutely crazy. Of course I'd like the million dollars but it's not worth harming my career for." Kylie has never been approached by any magazine to pose nude.

◀ Kylie was reported to have broken up the marriage of Aussie rock singer Greedy Smith of Mental as Anything, when in truth they have only met a couple of times during joint publicity engagements.

◀ Kylie hates her younger sister Dannii, also a singer and actress. Nothing could be further from the truth. The Minogues are a very close family and Kylie is over the moon about Dannii's achievements. Dannii even joined Kylie on her European promotional trip late last year.

◀ Kylie Should Be So Unlucky said one headline stating that Kylie had been spat on and sworn at by a mob of girls at the Hippodrome nightclub in London. Kylie was apparently rescued by her minders and "looked badly shaken". This story is totally untrue.

◄ "Kylie is anorexic". One magazine even printed Kylie's "confession" about suffering from the disease, her weight dropping to below 31 kg. The truth is that Kylie did lose weight during the hectic months when she was combining filming Neighbours and launching her musical career. With two full-time jobs, promotional activities and travelling around the world, there wasn't much time for leisurely meals. But Kylie has never suffered from anorexia – she has always been small and slim.

◄ Almost every week stories are printed about how much money Kylie is making. One week she's earning $2.5 million a month, the next she's negotiating a $15,000 a week deal to return to *Neighbours,* the next she's buying a multi-million dollar home somewhere. Kylie in fact doesn't know how much money she has earnt for the past few years of solid work. Her father Ron, an accountant, supervises her affairs, so at least she doesn't have to worry too much.

◄ One Melbourne newspaper even claimed Kylie was an alien! The "story" contained evidence from a French anthropologist about the appearance aliens might have and suggested Kylie bore an uncanny resemblance.

◄ Of course the media's on-again-off-again fascination with Kylie's relationship with good friend Jason Donovan continued to inspire loads of ridiculous stories. One moment Kylie had dumped Jason, the next they were getting married, the next Jason was seen with a "mystery brunette". Kylie and Jason's relationship is their own business, right!

Kylie accepts that her popularity means the media will always be dreaming up new stories to help sell newspapers. She takes all these rumours in her stride.

■ "Jason and I often get copies of press reports and joke about them," she laughs. "We say 'Wow, what have we done this week?' They haven't written I'm on heroin or that I'm pregnant yet. But after being an alien, who knows what's next?"

Carol Jones was a youngster when she emigrated with her parents to Australia from Maesteg in Wales. ■ The family settled in Townsville, Queensland and young Carol began ballet lessons. She had a natural talent and good looks, often winning trophies at the various contests she entered. She appeared at the Theatre Royal and seemed to have a promising future as a professional dancer. ■ "Basically I was shy. A bit quiet," she recalls. "I never really had the drive or ambition to go any further." ■ Perhaps another factor which determined the modest Carol's future was a certain Ron Minogue. When she was 20 Carol married and moved to Melbourne with Ron and began raising a family. ■ Their first child Kylie Ann was born on May 28 1968 at Melbourne's Bethlehem Hospital. Brother Brendan followed two years later, and sister Danielle the next year. ■ Kylie was a shy, small child, much more interested in sewing, handicrafts and swap cards than in playing pranks or leaping around sports fields. Both sisters learnt piano and had dance lessons — ballet, tap and jazz — although Carol says, "I was never very keen on them taking up dancing because it is such a hard life." ■ Mention singing however and Carol is lost for clues. "I have no idea where Kylie, or for that matter Dannii, got their singing ability. I can't even sing a note. I couldn't even sing in church!" ■ It wasn't until late in primary school that Kylie remembers becoming interested in performing. Disco music was all the rage at the time and Kylie loved dancing around the living room with a hairbrush for a microphone pretending she was in concert. ■ Sometimes she'd listen to her parents' records, The Beatles or The Rolling Stones, but usually she imitated popular artists and records of the time. ■ Kylie's acting career began when she was 11 and in her last year at primary school. A friend of Mrs Minogue was casting for a new television series at a production house called Crawfords and asked Danielle to audition. ■

To avoid the sisters arguing, Carol insisted Kylie be given the chance to audition too. And guess what? It turned out Danielle was too young and Kylie won the part. She played a Dutch girl, Carla, and had to learn to speak with a Netherlands accent. The series was called The Sullivans and went on to become one of the most acclaimed and popular series on Australian television. ■ Next up came a part for Kylie in Skyways playing a younger sister to . . . Jason Donovan! Kylie and Jason have remained good friends ever since. ■ Kylie's next major memory is of the film Grease starring Olivia Newton-John and John Travolta. Carol had taken all three children to see the musical, but it was Kylie who was most affected. ■ She admired the singing and dancing skills of the pretty Olivia, also an Australian, and quickly learnt the film's popular Greased Lightning dance. That one was displayed many a time around the Minogue living room.

Carol and Ron Minogue's wedding

Family holiday – 1969

Kylie was also a big fan of the Swedish pop stars Abba, a major musical force in the mid '70s. Kylie loved to imitate "the blonde one", copying the group's movements from TV videos and with friends staged Abba concerts at home. Living room concerts aside, Kylie was pretty much your average teenager. She was a good school student, not brilliant, preferring Art, Graphics and Human Development to Maths. She enjoyed family life and formed close friendships with several girls who remain her best friends to this day.

On Sundays she worked behind the counter at the local video shop, and with school nearing an end, wondered what the future held. Then came a timely break. In 1984, five years after her last acting job, Kylie was invited for another audition. The part she eventually won was of Charlotte Kernow in a popular series The Henderson Kids. Kylie loved the Charlotte character, a tough, streetwise kid who was to be in the show for six months. The only problem was that filming would continue until March 1985, a few months into the last all-important year of school study, called the Higher School Certificate. Determined to play the part, Kylie arranged to have a tutor on set and crammed in school work in breaks and at night. She still remembers it was difficult resuming school two months into the year, meeting classmates and teachers for the first time and re-adjusting to life as a schoolgirl.

Danielle and Kylie – 1980

Baby Kylie

Kylie the animal lover

The highly regarded Henderson Kids series gave Kylie another chance to contemplate a future as an actress. During the year she picked up two other small parts, and by year end she was convinced it was the future she wanted. She also managed to pass her HSC and during the Christmas break did some long, hard thinking about the decision she had made. ■ "I knew I wanted to do more acting but I really was scared of not being able to get work," she says. "I was being more concerned than I needed to be as it turns out but it could easily have been difficult. For a time I was thinking of doing a secretarial course just to have something there."

KYLIE A BIOGRAPHY

The practical, conservative side of Kylie's nature left her fully aware of the insecurities and frustrations of the acting profession, still she felt she was young enough to give it a try. ▪ First she secured an acting agent and before she had time to have second doubts, an audition for a TV series called Neighbours came up. A week later in February 1986, she was Charlene Mitchell. ▪ No one, least of all Kylie, could ever have imagined what the next few years would bring. ▪ Firstly it meant revamping her lifestyle. With the alarm ringing at 6.15am and lines to memorise the night before, late nights were out. On the plus side, producing 2½ hours of television a week gave Kylie an ideal opportunity to learn about acting, an education she believes will stand her in good stead for future roles. ▪ As Neighbours grew in popularity, things like spending time with friends, travelling and hobbies became almost an impossibility, but there was more. ▪ Suddenly, Kylie was famous. Everywhere she went people recognised her, asked for autographs and wondered what Charlene would be up to in future episodes. She was flooded with interview and photo requests, trips interstate for promotion — she was now living a public life. ▪ In March 1987, just one year after joining Neighbours, came proof of Kylie's amazing popularity. She became the youngest person ever to win the Most Popular Actress at the Australian Television Awards, the Logies. She accepted the award in a striking red leather skirt she made herself. ▪ By 1988 Kylie had rocketed to stardom around the world, and the media re-named that year's television awards the "Minogies". Kylie became the first person to win four Logies in one night — Australia's Most Popular Television Personality, Victoria's Most Popular Personality, Most Popular Actress (the second year running) and Most Popular Musical Video (Locomotion).

It was an amazing achievement that may never be bettered.

■ Since leaving Neighbours in mid 1988, Kylie has concentrated on her singing career, and has notched up awards of the musical variety.

■ Despite all these successes, Kylie still says quite honestly "I'm still a normal Aussie. I may have the success, but to me I'm still me. I've still got my own problems and hang ups and these sorts of things. ■ I still go home to Mum and she cooks the dinner. That's why home is so important to me. I mean there's this big career exposure, but then I can go home and I'm a nobody. You can be your usual dag self. ■ I just potter at home, making little things, sewing. It's great — you don't have to smile or anything!"

■ ■ ■ ■ ■
NEIGHBOURS

In 1989 the *Neighbours* success story has gone marching on. ■ Newspapers and magazines on both sides of the globe are still packed with *Neighbours* articles, the show's stars Kylie and Jason have rocketed to stardom and it seems almost everyone in Britain dashes home to be in front of the telly by 5.35 p.m. ■ School children, career women, pop stars, families — latest reports suggest that up to 20 million Brits are now addicted! And included in those are the Royal Family. Yes, from the Queen Mum to Princess Di, the Royals are keen fans, so much so that they specially requested the *Neighbours* cast to perform at last November's Royal Variety Performance. ■ This Christmas retailers are again expecting the *Neighbours* board game to outsell all comers, and just ask the Sunday Mirror how popular *Neighbours* competitions are. The paper had to hire an extra 20 staff to cope with the avalanche of entries for a contest to visit Australia and meet the cast. The paper reported more than one million entries in the first three days. ■ The programme's phenomenal popularity peaked early in 1989 with the wedding of Charlene and Scott. The marriage theme song *Suddenly* by Angry Anderson leapt to the top of the charts (making Angry not very angry at all!). It was undoubtedly one of the television highlights of the year, just as it had been in Australia. ■ Down Under *Neighbours* is in its third year as King of the Soapies. The wedding even made the cover of Time magazine. It again swept the pool at the Australian television awards, the Logies, and has consistently broken records in TV ratings.

Unfortunately for the cast it is now becoming difficult to appear in public without being mobbed. ■ *Neighbours* even made it into Melbourne's top museum. For five months from August 1988 the Performing Arts Museum had a *Neighbours* exhibition, showing how episodes are made, videos of interviews with the cast and crew, producers and writers, historical background and education information on sound, editing, etc. It was a great success and quite an honour for the programme. ■ As we move toward 1990, *Neighbours* shows no signs of dropping in popularity even though Kylie is now off screen. And that's something that has pleased her greatly.

BEHIND THE SUCCESS?

Everyone has their own idea why *Neighbours* is so entertaining, but perhaps the most authoritative person to ask is the show's creator, Reg Watson. ■ Reg produced Britain's Crossroads for ten years, before returning to his native Australia to work on various top serials such as Sons and Daughters. ■ Simply, Reg says, *Neighbours* is about ordinary people going about their ordinary lives, and as such viewers of all ages can comfortably relate to it. No wild sensationalism, no rapes, murders or violence, no ridiculous plots are wanted. ■ "Anything that happens in an average street will happen in the serial," he explains. "I came to the conclusion that the 'heavy' in *Neighbours* is life itself and once you accept that, it opens up everything. The show's simplicity is where its strength is." ■ Kylie adds another important point: "In most things we do there is an underlying moral aspect. It's not preaching to the kids. We're not telling them what to do. It's just showing the outcome of various situations which will hopefully help them." ■ Reg also confesses he considered calling the show One Way Street or No Through Road, but, "In the end it came down to being what it is, a story about neighbours."

NEIGHBOURS IN BRITAIN

Ramsay Street first entered British lives in October 1986 at 1.30 p.m. which was really rather silly because most of the potential viewers were at school or work. ■ But in January 1988 a clever BBC man decided to repeat it at 5.35 p.m. each day and in just a few months, its audience was 14 million and growing fast. ■ Soon it was topping Coronation Street and East Enders which the TV critics couldn't understand at all. One branded *Neighbours* "the cheapest brand of soap on the market". Another said, "It has the production qualities of a badly lit home movie . . but it doesn't seem to matter, the Brits are hooked."

So hooked that in 1988 when Prince Charles and Lady Diana visited Australia, dozens of British photographers were dashing off at every available moment to the Channel 10 studios to shoot anything that moved to meet the demand back home.

■ These days the Channel 10 Melbourne studios continue to receive sacks of fan mail daily, but now they have airmail stickers all over them.

■ Just for the record, British episodes are more than 18 months behind the Australian ones, so unless you want to peep into the future, don't speak to anyone who's been Down Under on holiday!

Kylie joined *Neighbours* in February 1986, just after finishing school. ■ The part of the feisty tomboy motor mechanic Charlene Mitchell was originally for 12 weeks only. Charlene had come to Ramsay Street to visit her mother, fed up with living with her father in another state. She loves cars and quickly got an apprenticeship with Rob at the garage. ■ The character proved so popular with Aussie audiences, Kylie's contract was extended and extended and extended. The ups and downs of her relationship with boyfriend Scott Robinson (Jason Donovan) became one of the major attractions of the show. ■ On a typical *Neighbours* day, Kylie wakes at 6 a.m. to be in the studio by 6.45 a.m. After hair and make-up, Kylie is on and off set all day, sometimes till 7 p.m. ■ Then it's home, dinner with the family, learn the next day's lines and into bed. On weekends and the more quiet studio days, there are photo sessions, interviews, personal appearances, fan mail to answer and promotions in other states. ■ With *Neighbours,* Kylie often averaged a 60 to 70 hour week, so as she often says, "Don't let anyone tell you television is all glamour!"

THE WEDDING

Two particular memories come to mind when Kylie thinks of Charlene's highly publicised wedding to Scott. ■ The day before the episode screened on Australian TV, Kylie and Jason attended a Sydney shopping centre to promote it. More than 4000 fans crammed the area, with several hundred people injured in the hysteria. Police and security guards had to whisk the pair away. ■ It was a frightening experience and undeniable proof of how powerful the programme had become. ■ "It was a little difficult to understand," Kylie recalls. "I'd have people come up to me thinking I was really getting married. ■ "They were so excited and their whole lives seemed to be revolving around it. People look up to you so much and I stop and think why? ■ "I'm just a normal person and it's a bit frightening in a way that they're all watching everything you do." ■ Kylie's other main memory was how difficult the wedding scene actually was to shoot. ■ "It was a really tiring day. I must have walked up and down that aisle 20 times while we were trying to capture the right mood, the right lights and all that." ■ Spending 10 hours in the wedding dress, reshooting and reshooting until everything was absolutely perfect made for stunning television viewing, but definitely one of Kylie's hardest days.

Leaving *Neighbours* in July 1988 after 2½ years was one of the toughest decisions Kylie has ever had to make. ■ With her recording career taking off, continual demands from overseas for publicity trips and videos and albums to be made, the workload became impossible to manage. ■ "The hardest part of the decision is to get across that I'm not snobbing people," Kylie stresses. "I'm not leaving because I think I'm too good for the job. I feel I have to devote my time to other things now. After all, I can't hang on to *Neighbours* forever." ■ After a few marital hiccups, Charlene leaves the show when her grandfather gives her and Scott a house in Brisbane. Scott stays in Erinsborough until he can arrange another journalism job and follow her. The script is left open-ended so Kylie has the chance to return to the series in the future. ■ "I thought my last day would be emotional and it was. I bawled my eyes out," she laughs. "At my farewell party I tried to make a speech and I burst into tears again. ■ "I don't think anyone understood a word I said through all the sniffling and mumbling. I really will miss all the cast members."

A DAY ON THE NEIGHBOURS SET

About thirty minutes drive from the centre of Melbourne through modest suburban houses and you're at Channel 10, the home of *Neighbours*. ■ Most afternoons there's a swag of teenagers from the nearby high school outside hoping for a glimpse or an autograph from one of the stars. ■ Through the security check, down a long corridor and into Studio B and voila . . . we've stepped into the *Neighbours* world. Yes, there's the coffee shop, Mrs Mangel's loungeroom, the Robinsons' kitchen. ■ The studio is absolutely huge, with rows and rows of lights hanging from the roof. Most of the rooms on the show are left permanently standing, with just one or two changed each couple of days. ■ Today is one of the week's three rehearsal days which means no lights, no cameras, no make-up and casual clothes. It's just the actors and the director practising lines, timing and movements over and over again until the scene is perfect for the next day's recording. ■ Three cameramen also follow the action lining up camera angles. In the breaks they chat happily about what they did on the weekend, the results of the Australian Rules football games and so on. As it is a rehearsal day, everything seems quite relaxed. ■ There are 20 or so scenes to go through each day, so the cast are often at the studio by 7 a.m. and some may not leave until the evening. ■ On the set Kylie is rehearsing a scene with Jason Donovan in the coffee shop. Director Steve Mann talks quietly to them, suggesting different phrasing or actions, repeating the same 30 second scene five or six times. ■ "G'day mate. How are ya?" A cheerful voice beckons from the studio door. The cast jester Craig McLachlan (Henry Mitchell) comes bounding in. Craig is what you'd call a zany type of guy. Already the cameramen are grinning as he launches into a series of new jokes, animating wildly.

He spots Kylie who's quietly trying to revise her lines. "Shut up Minogue. Stop making so much noise," he says sternly, which of course cracks Kylie up. ■ The *Neighbours* cast are all great mates, encouraging and supporting each other, making the long day's schedules as enjoyable as possible. ■ As Kylie says: "If you tried to have a day without joking on the set I think we'd all die because they are such long hours and there really is a lot of pressure. We try to make the best of it. It keeps us all going." ■ A couple of Props Department boys carry in some furniture to be added to the next scene, which allows time for a quick chat with the floor manager, Ray Lindsay. ■ "As the director's mouthpiece on the floor, I have to know how to handle everyone's little moods, to be a diplomat and sometimes pick when to treat them a little more gently," he explains. "They all have their moments but it's a good cast to work with. We've never had any animosity or fights on the set. Work is the important thing." ■ Anne Charleston (Madge Mitchell) appears on set for a scene with Craig. Kylie and Jason head to the canteen for an extremely late lunch. The station's Publicity Manager arrives with a journalist for yet another interview, this time with Annie Jones (Jane Harris). ■ Around the wardrobe area new clothes are being made for Fiona Corke (Gail Lewis). Each character has his/her own hanging rack of clothes from which the actor may wear what they like. ■ With special events like weddings, the wardrobe department are kept busy buying, altering and making clothes to suit the characters.

A normal *Neighbours* week consists of two days rehearsals (lines having been learnt at home beforehand), two to three days recording in the studio and two to three days location recording. The episodes are filmed about six weeks ahead. ■ The actual location of Ramsay Street is a fiercely kept secret. With all the activity involved in an outside shoot — technical production workers, caterers, make-up ladies, hairdressers etc — there's no time to be wasted with hordes of onlookers. ■ Back in the studio Jamie is wailing his head off while poor old "father" Paul Keane (Des) and the director wait to rehearse a scene. ■ There's never a dull moment in Studio B, but for all the fun and frivolity, it's plain hard work that has made *Neighbours* such a successful soapie.

"Kylie's appeal is universal. She's everything every young girl want to be — bright, fresh and cheerful. Fashions move so quickly but if she really sticks at it, she has the talent to become one of the great entertainers of the world. ■ "She has a great voice. I love working with her because she has a terrific sense of humour, a fabulous personality and she knows how to really sell a song." ■ High praise indeed, but even more so coming from top record producer Mike Stock. With his partners Matt Aitken and Pete Waterman, the trio have made recording history as the most successful hit-makers of the '80s. ■ Producing artists such as Rick Astley, Bananarama and Mel and Kim, the SAW team have sold more than 56 million records worldwide. In 1990 they continue a seemingly endless run of number one singles and albums. ■ Kylie Minogue is the team's most successful artist. In 1988 she was the biggest selling rock music artist in Britain with the number one album and five singles in the Top 20. ■ This year that success has continued, firstly with the Kylie/Jason Donovan duet *Especially For You*, the April single *Hand On Your Heart* and Kylie's second album, just released. ■ And to think all this sprang from an impromptu jam session by the Neighbours cast at a benefit for an Australian Rules football team! That night the crowd so loved Kylie's unrehearsed rendition of *Locomotion*, she was encouraged to record it. ■ By mid 1987 it was Australia's number one single and went on to become the best-selling single of the year. ■ "To be honest I was very surprised at its success," Kylie says in retrospect. "I've always loved singing but at the time I was happy to be trying something new, something that identified me as someone apart from Charlene." ■ The Mushroom Records Australian label then arranged for the famous Stock, Aitken and Waterman to write and produce Kylie's next single — *I Should Be So Lucky*.

Stock, Aitken
and Waterman

With a vibrant film clip behind it, *Lucky* proved irresistible. It hit the top spot in Britain in March 1988 making Kylie the first artist ever to hold simultaneous number ones in Britain and Australia. *Lucky* went on to sell more than two million copies and topped the charts worldwide. This included an incredible twelve weeks on top in Japan. ■ Six months later the Kylie album debuted at number two in both Britain and Australia, the highest debut LP by a female in either country. Later that month Kylie became the first Australian artist to hold a number one UK album. The album eventually hit the number one position in 15 countries! ■ By this time Kylie's Neighbours partner Jason Donovan had scored his own first hit with *Nothing Can Divide Us*. Fans began to press for a duet. ■ "The idea of a duet was taboo for a long time," Kylie says. "We were always dead against the idea, but PWL (the UK record company) were telling us they had thousands of pre-orders for this song that no one had ever spoken or heard about. So I guess we've done it because of public demand." ■ With the Christmas season rapidly approaching, time was of the essence. Pete Waterman and Matt Aitken dashed to Australia arriving November 9. They spent the next 36 hours in a Sydney studio with Kylie and Jason, and with the finished tapes under their arms, rushed back on to a London-bound plane. ■ The *Especially For You* video was shot in the next few days, unfortunately in some of the worst weather conditions Sydney has seen. One day recorded the coldest November temperature in 100 years! ■ "I can laugh about it now," Kylie says, "but we were exhausted by the end of it. We spent the whole next week recovering." ■ The single was released in Britain on November 28. The big question was would it make the prestigious Christmas number one spot? ■ Kylie and Jason hurried to London for some last minute promotion, but alas, they were pipped by Cliff Richard's *Mistletoe and Wine*.

Kylie's consolation was notching up the highest selling UK album of the year (six times platinum) and still at number two after six months of release. ■ Her 1989 New Year's present came when *Especially For You* hit number one on January 20. ■ In February it was back to London to record three new songs, the *Hand On Your Heart* single and B-side and a possible LP track. *Hand On Your Heart*, released in April, carried on her phenomenal singles success. ■ It was time to begin thinking of a new album and in June Kylie headed back to London to begin recording, again with Stock, Aitken and Waterman. With one album behind her and much more experience, Kylie was enthusiastic about her input into the project and coming up with a great new set of songs. ■ Wiser, and more relaxed, Kylie feels she has never sung better and is confident album number two will prove more popular and accomplished than her debut. ■ With a September release, judge for yourself.

KYLIE'S CAREER HIGHLIGHTS

◄ **1980**
First professional acting role in "Skyways".

◄ **1981**
Role in "The Sullivans".

◄ **1984 / 5**
Role in "The Henderson Kids".

◄ **1986**
Kylie leaves school and accepts role of Charlene in "Neighbours".

◄ **1987**
"Neighbours" becomes Australia's highest rating programme.

◄ **MARCH 1987**
Kylie becomes the youngest star ever to win the Silver Logie for "Most Popular Actress in Australia".

Kylie mobbed at Sydney shopping centre.

◄ **JULY 1987**
Release of Kylie's first single, a remake of the '60s Little Eva hit "Locomotion".

◄ **AUGUST 1987**
"Locomotion" hits No. 1 nationally around Australia and remains there for seven weeks.

◄ **SEPTEMBER 1987**
"Locomotion" goes platinum. Kylie teams up with famed record producers Stock, Aitken and Waterman in London.

◄ **OCTOBER 1987**
"Neighbours" becomes one of the highest rating programmes in the U.K.

"Locomotion" sets records as the biggest Australian single of the decade.

◄ **NOVEMBER 1987**
"Locomotion" becomes Mushroom Records first international No. 1 by topping the charts in New Zealand and Hong Kong.

◄ **JANUARY 1988**
Release of "I Should Be So Lucky" in U.K. and Australia.

Performance before Prince Charles and the Princess Diana for the Australian Royal Bicentennial Concert.

◄ **FEBRUARY 1988**
Kylie presented with award from the Australian Record Industry Association for "Locomotion" being the highest selling record of 1987.

◄ **MARCH 1988**
Kylie becomes first ever to win 4 Logies on one night: the Gold for "Most Popular Personality on Australian Television", the Silver for the second year in a row, "Most Popular Personality in Victorian (state) Television" and "Most Popular Music Video in Australia" for "Locomotion". She is the youngest actor/actress ever to hold five Logies (the Australian equivalent to Emmys).

"I Should Be So Lucky" sets records in U.K. as first single for over 10 years to stay at No. 1 for five weeks. "I Should Be So Lucky" becomes the biggest selling single in the U.K. in 1988 (sales in Britain over 675,000, worldwide, well over the million mark).

With "I Should Be So Lucky" Kylie became the first artist ever to hold simultaneous No. 1s in Australia and Britain (14 March).

◄ APRIL 1988

"I Should Be So Lucky" goes platinum in Australia staying at No. 1 for five weeks.

"I Should Be So Lucky" No. 1 in Germany (3 weeks), Finland, Israel, Switzerland and Hong Kong, as well as top 5 positions in Austria, Denmark, Norway, Belgium, Spain, Italy, Greece, France and New Zealand.

"I Should Be So Lucky" enters Billboard Top 100 with a bullet the week after release in the U.S., peaking at No. 28 giving Kylie her first Top 40 hit in the U.S.

◄ MAY 1988

Having sold over 1 million copies in Europe, "I Should Be So Lucky" stays atop Pan-European charts for 3 weeks.

◄ JUNE 1988

Third single "Got To Be Certain" released in England entering the charts at No. 15 and spending six weeks at the No. 2 spot.

◄ JULY 1988

"I Should Be So Lucky" reaches No. 1 in Japan and holds that position for twelve weeks.

"Got To Be Certain" creates history by being the first record in Australia to debut at No. 1 on the national charts; it stayed there for five weeks. No. 1 in Hong Kong, Israel, New Zealand and Finland, and Top 10 in Germany, Austria, Switzerland, Denmark, Spain and Norway.

The fastest start to a career in Europe with three Top 10 records in the first seven months of 1988 plus a platinum album in just four weeks in the U.K.

◄ AUGUST 1988

"The Locomotion" debuts on the British charts (1 August) at No. 2, giving Kylie the record for the highest entry on the U.K. single charts by a female artist, a record previously held by Madonna when she entered at No. 3.

The album "Kylie" debuts at No. 2 in both Britain and Australia. Never before has a debut album by a female artist entered so high on either country's charts. On release it went double platinum in Australia, gold in Britain and gold in Singapore.

The album hits No. 1 in England (21 August) and stays there for 4 weeks. Already platinum in U.K. and gold in Germany. Also Top 10 throughout Europe and Asia.

■ ■ ■ ■ ■

SEPTEMBER 1988
"The Locomotion" hits the U.S. Top 40 on 14 September with a bullet and goes to the No. 1 spot on the Eurochart only 3 weeks after release.

Readers of the London Sun voted Kylie No. 1 Girl Singer and the Top Newcomer!

OCTOBER 1988
Kylie's fourth British single "Je Ne Sais Pas Pourquoi", debuted at No. 2 and stayed there for 3 weeks, giving her the record of being the first artist in the history of the British charts to have 4 top three singles from one album. U.K. Smash Hits readers voted her Most Fanciable Female and Best Female Singer.

NOVEMBER 1988
"The Locomotion" reached No. 3 on the American charts, with sales there in excess of ½ million.

The album "Kylie" returns to No. 1 in England (15 November) making it 8 weeks at No. 1. British sales pass the 1.2 million mark (quadruple platinum) making "Kylie" the biggest selling album of the year.

Her duet with Jason Donovan, "Especially For You" debuted at No. 2 and shipped Silver on release, making Kylie the first female artist to have her first five singles all go silver. This brought Kylie's single sales in the U.K. to well over 2 million, and her first video album, released the same week, debuted at No. 1 and sold in excess of double platinum within 3 weeks. Kylie has her 3rd U.S. hit when "It's No Secret" charts in the U.S. on the week of release (hitting the U.S. Top 40 25 January, 1989).

Kylie performs at the Royal Variety Show in London before the Queen Mother.

DECEMBER 1988
"I Should Be So Lucky" receives "Record of the Year" award at the coveted "Japanese Popular Disc Awards".

Kylie becomes the first artist ever in Finland to have 4 consecutive No. 1 singles.

Australian Smash Hits readers voted her "Most Fanciable Female Singer" and "Best Female Singer", whilst readers of the Australian Magazine TV Hits voted her "Hunkiest Person Alive" and "Best Female TV Personality".

In Israel Kylie is the only artist to end the year with three singles in the Top 40. She is voted "Most Popular Female Singer of the Year".

Kylie ends the year in the U.K. with the biggest album of 1988 (6 times platinum with sales of 1.8 million) at No. 2 (having been in the top 10 since its release in June); No. 1 video, and No. 2 single, "Especially For You" with Jason Donovan.

◄ **J A N U A R Y   1 9 8 9**

Kylie signed to star in feature film entitled "The Delinquents" co-produced by David Bowie.

"Especially For You" goes No. 1 in U.K.

"Turn It Into Love" goes No. 1 on Japanese International chart. Kylie's third consecutive Japanese No. 1 and the sixth single from the album.

"Locomotion" goes No. 1 in Canada, giving her three simultaneous No. 1s internationally.

Kylie is No. 1 in the Record Mirror survey of the top recording acts of 1988 in the U.K., compiled from sales information of over 40,000 different records, collected by Gallup.

◄ **F E B R U A R Y   1 9 8 9**

"Especially For You" hits Top 10 in Germany.

Kylie voted "Best International Female Artist" by a landslide in Irish Record Industry Awards.

The Japanese Phonographic Record Association presents Kylie with two 1988 "Disc Awards" for "The Best Selling New Artist" and "Best Selling Single of the Year" ("I Should Be So Lucky").

"Kylie" the album turns gold in the U.S.A.

"Especially For You" goes No. 1 in Hong Kong — staying there for six weeks!

Kylie becomes one of the honoured few to pose for a wax model of herself at the world famous Madame Tussaud's in London.

The Mirror in London voted Kylie best actress in the world!

The Music Week awards in London awarded Kylie No. 1 independent single of 1988 for "I Should Be So Lucky" and No. 1 video.

◄ **M A R C H   1 9 8 9**

The Australian Record Industry Association nominates Kylie for five awards with "I Should Be So Lucky" picking up Biggest Selling Single of the Year (1988).

Kylie dominates the Japanese international charts with five singles in the top 40, three of them in the top four. "Turn It Into Love" is number one for the 10th week running.

Kylie accepts her second award from the Variety Club of Australia for Recording Artist of the Year.

◄ **A P R I L   1 9 8 9**

"Hand On Your Heart" released in U.K. and Australia.

Kylie begins rehearsals for her first feature film "The Delinquents".

WORLD CHART PLACINGS

	AUSTRALIA	AUSTRIA	BELGIUM	CANADA	DENMARK	EUROCHART	FINLAND	FRANCE	GERMANY	GREECE	HOLLAND	HONG KONG
I Should Be So Lucky	1	4	1	25	5	1	1	4	1	2	12	1
Got To Be Certain	1	14	1		6	2	1	9	6		28	1
Locomotion	1	6	1	1	5	1	1	6	3		6	1
Je Ne Sais Pas Pourquoi	11	14	3		16		1		14		47	4
Especially For You	2		1						13		4	1
It's No Secret				22								
Kylie L.P.	2	18	4	10	5		6	28	9		12	1

	IRELAND	ISRAEL	ITALY	JAPAN (Int'l)	N. ZEALAND	NORWAY	PORTUGAL	SWEDEN	SWITZERLAND	SPAIN	U. KINGDOM	AMERICA
I Should Be So Lucky	1	1	6	1	2	3		12	1	3	1	28
Got To Be Certain		1	37	10	3	4		3	8	9	2	
Locomotion	1	1		1	3	3	6	3	2	7	2	3
Je Ne Sais Pas Pourquoi		7			8			24			2	
Especially For You	1			3							1	
It's No Secret				4								37
Kylie L.P.	1	7		4	1	4	1	13	7		1	53

EMPLOYMENT PROHIBITED

IMMIGRATION OFFICER
(712)
19 OCT 1987
HEATHROW (3)

日 本 国 査 証
VISA（ 短 ）
Good for ...multiple... journey ...to
Japan ...for tourism
within ...twelve... months of
...eof if passport remains
...bourne OCT. 15 1988
...the Consul-Gene...

JAPAN CONSULATE-GENERAL · MELBOURNE

AUSTRALIA
27 MAR 1988
73
MELBOURNE AIRPORT

KYLIE MINOGUE

JULY 1

... Making her Asian Debut to celebrate the release of her first Album ...

UK #1 I Should Be So Lucky

UK #2 Got to Be Certain

Australia #1 Locomotion

Midnight Show at CANTON July 1

Non Members $88 Members $44

Call today for reservations: 3-7210209

KYLIE MINOGUE 宣傳她首張個人大碟，巡迴亞洲演唱。

Tickets on sale now at Canton

KYLIE MINOGUE WILL BE APPEARING LIVE IN PERSON AT CANTON. HER SHOW WILL CONSIST OF A LIVE SINGING PERFORMANCE BACKED BY A RECORDED MUSIC TRACK. THE SHOW WILL BE AT LEAST 30 MINUTES LONG AND WILL INCLUDE KYLIE'S THREE INTERNATIONAL HITS PLUS ADDITIONAL SONGS FROM HER FORTHCOMING DEBUT ALBUM. KYLIE IS ONE OF THE WORLD'S LEADING YOUNG PERFORMERS. SUCCESSFULLY JUGGLING HER SINGING AND BURGEONING CAREER AS THE STAR OF THE UK'S LEADING SOAP SERIES NEIGHBOURS - EXPECT A NIGHT OF MAGIC FROM THIS MULTI-TALENTED PERFORMER!!

KYLIE MINOGUE 在舉著的土張個人現場演唱
她將唱三十分鐘以上，由表替錄音帶伴唱其
歌將唱出首張個人大碟其中三首選曲及少數
門歌曲

KYLIE 是世界上其中一個年惡記唱演出表
...此寵歌名利成功地獲轉了她的歌出及
...英國最受歡迎的劇中的一類著角，是她一
...統實利得各不着動如現望白的演出！

COMING SOON:
3rd Anniversary : July 15
...esi & Shirlie : July 16 & 17

time to eat

okay gang, this is the cooking section.
Now, see if you can raid Mum's pantry, or
if you've got a crush on the hunk next door,
this is the 'perfect excuse' to borrow a cup of
something! Either way, here are a couple of
my favourite recipes.

☀ —— Oriental Fish —— ☀ serves 4.

This dish is really quick & easy — healthy too'.

4 fish fillets (flounder, sole)
1 carrot, julienned
3 spring onions with tops, julienned
  fresh ginger to taste
2 tbsp parsley, minced
2 tbsp vinegar (rice)
2 tbsp light soy sauce
1 tbsp lemon juice
2 tsp sesame oil

Lay the fillets on a heat-proof plate — spread
veggies over the top. Mix vinegar, soy sauce,
lemon juice & sesame oil together — pour
over fish. Put another heat-proof plate into
a large, deep skillet (something the fish plate
can sit on and be off the bottom). Add about
an inch of water to skillet. Put fish plate
into pan. Cover & steam 7-10 mins. Serve ☀♡
You can cook this in a frying pan if you like'.

So, your meal is done & you feel like some dessert. Here are two, which are really simple.

⁃ ── Rice Pudding ── ⁃

An 'oldy' but a 'goody' my Grandma used to make this for us. Gas 3/170°C/325°F Serves 6.

2 c. cooked brown rice   1/4 c. brown sugar
3 c. whole milk   1 c. raisins
1/2 tsp mixed cinnamon & nutmeg
3 eggs beaten

Beat eggs in a large bowl. Add remaining ingredients, mix well. Pour into greased casserole dish. Bake at 325° for about 1 hour, or until set. Serve hot or cold with whipped cream if you like ♡♡

⁃ ── Kiwi Ice ── ⁃

For those with a 'sweet tooth'. Serves 4.

4 Kiwi fruit (keep perfect slice for each serve)
5 tbsp fresh lemon or lime juice
1/4 tbsp grated lemon rind   1 c. water
1/2 c. sugar   1/2 c. light corn syrup

Purée fruit, juice and rind in blender. Cook water, sugar & corn syrup until sugar dissolves. Mix all together & pour in shallow pan. Refrigerate, in freezer for 1 1/2 hours. Take out and beat till light & fluffy. Freeze another 2 hours. Serve in glasses 🍸, garnish with kiwi slice & fresh sprigs of mint or pineapple ⚘⚘◉ ♡.

A C R O S S :

1. Kylie's first recording and first Australian hit. (10)

8. The Neighbours street. (6)

12. Kylie's interest in this has certainly helped her career. (7)

13. A popular film of yesteryear. (2)

15. Kylie's records usually top the ————. (5)

16. How old was Kylie in 1976? (4)

17. It's —— Secret. (2)

18. Kylie's home. (9)

19. Something that is stuck on records. (5)

21. Do the locomotion with ——. (2)

22. Kylie released her second one of these in 1989. (5)

26. Kylie's producers. (3)

28. Kylie's one-eyed sister. (5)

30. British Magazine Number ———. (3)

31. Kylie's schedule is full of these. (10)

33. Melbourne, Australia has this unusual form of transport. (5)

35. What Kylie wears in France. (5)

39. Where records are produced. (6)

41. Kylie sings with this. (5)

42. One of Kylie's favourite singers, jumbled up. (7)

43. Small word. (2)

44. Charlene and Scott exchanged these on their wedding day. (5)

46. British Magazine ——— Face. (3)

48. Charlene's mother, backwards. (5)

50. One of Kylie's favourite pastimes is to ————. (4)

52. One of Kylie's favourite foods is ————late. (5)

53. Wembley ————. (5)

55. You use your ears to ————. (4)

57. —— —— Sais Pas Pourquoi. (2,2)

58. The suburb where Neighbours is set is ————sborough, jumbled up. (4)

59. British and French Magazine. (4)

60. Where you might see Kylie. (2)

61. The beginning of a song. (5)

63. One ridiculous rumour about Kylie is that she is ———— $50 million dollars! (5)

64. European Economic Community. (3)

65. Kylie is certainly a ————. (4)

67. One of Kylie's nicknames. (7)

68. Kylie and Jason sang one. (4)

70. Kylie's brother. (7)

CROSSWORD

DOWN:

1. I Should Be So ————. (5)
2. Kylie's character in Neighbours. (8)
3. A form of music Kylie doesn't sing is heavy ————. (5)
4. Los Angeles is often called ———— town. (6)
5. Top —— The Pops. (2)
6. Greek singer ———— Mouskouri. (4)
7. A type of food Kylie likes. (4)
8. Kylie's dad. (3)
9. A koala is an Australian —————. (6)
10. Each Neighbours episode is made up of a variety of —————. (6)
11. The currency Kylie spends while in Japan. (3)
14. Top British TV pop show. (4)
20. Los Angeles. (2)
21. Scott and Charlene are now ——— and wife. (3)
23. Sunny city in Australia. (8)
24. Charlene's profession. (5,8)
25. Kylie's favourite brand of jeans. (4)
27. A highlight of Neighbours was Scott and Charlene's —————. (7)
28. Jason who? (7)
29. A country where Kylie has had great success. (6)
32. One of Kylie's famous producers. (8)
34. Charlene's family. (8)
36. Abbreviation for the person who runs a magazine. (2)
37. Je —— Sais Pas, backwards. (2)
38. Got —— —— —————. (2,2,7)
40. A nightclub activity. (5)
45. Kylie appears regularly in this magazine. (5,4)
47. Hand on Your ————. (5)
49. A 60 s style of dancing, go ——. (2)
51. One of Kylie's favourite actors, surname. (7)
54. It can be 7in. 12in, EP and LP. (6)
56. One of Kylie's favourite actors, first name of 31 down. (5)
62. Abbreviation for overseas. (2)
63. Western Australia. (2)
66. Something you get in Australia. (3)
67. Got To —— Certain. (2)
69. Jason's hit, Nothing Can Divide ——. (2)

SOLUTION:

ACROSS: 1 Locomotion, 8 Ramsay, 12 Fashion, 13 ET, 15 chart, 16 nine, 17 No, 18 Australia, 19 label, 21 me, 22 album, 26 SAW, 28 Danni, 30 One, 31 interviews, 33 trams, 35 beret, 39 studio, 41 voice, 42 nadmnoa, 43 an, 44 rings, 46 The, 48 egdaM, 50 shop, 52 choco, 53 Arena, 55 hear, 57 Je Ne, 58 rien, 59 Ellie, 60 TV, 61 intro, 63 worth, 64 EEC, 65 star, 67 Bruiser, 68 duet, 70 Brendan.

FILL IN THE BLANKS
AND MAKE UP YOUR OWN KYLIE STORY

IT'S EASY!

When Kylie arrived in England, it was _Summer_ and so it was _hot_

Thank goodnes she packed her _sunglasses_. At the airport there were lots of _people_

so she dashed to the _car_ and was off. That afternoon she went _out_

to _shop_ and bought _sweats_ for herself and some _perfume_ for her mum.

A quick _drink_ and it was time to get ready to appear on _~~perfume~~ stage_. At the

television studio she met _Jason_ and _Craig_ and had a good old chat

about _~~cat~~ neighbours_. Soon it was time for her performance. Kylie

sang _I should be so lucky_ and everyone commented on her clothes, a _dress_ with _high heels_.

The next day after dreaming about _~~see~~ music_, Kylie had an interview at Radio One

on the _pop_ show. _~~She~~ Henry_ asked Kylie about her _songs_ and played _them_.

For the next _few_ weeks Kylie toured around Europe from _place_ to

place doing _shows_ and appearing on _tv_.

Her new album _realy_ was shooting up the _charts_ so it was

a _great_ time. Her favourite country was _Britain_ because

she liked the _~~Sun~~ people_. She rang home at night regularly to speak to

mum. The thing she missed most about Australia was _Sun_.

But all in all she had a _good_ trip and knew she'd be back again soon.

KYLIE

I Should Be So Lucky
Special U.K. Remix

I SHOULD BE
SO LUCKY 12"
United Kingdom
and Germany

KYLIE – THE ALBUM
The world

KYLIE MINOGUE
I SHOULD BE SO LUCKY

THE BICENTENNIAL
200
REMIX

I SHOULD BE SO LUCKY 12"
Australia

KYLIE

LOCO
MOTION
CHUGGA-MOTION MIX

LOCOMOTION 12"
Australia

I SHOULD BE SO LUCKY
Australia

I SHOULD BE SO LUCKY
France

I SHOULD BE SO LUCKY
Japan

I SHOULD BE SO LUCKY
United Kingdom

THE KYLIE COLLECTION – ALBUM
Australia

GOT TO BE CERTAIN 12"
Germany

GOT TO BE CERTAIN
Most of the world

THE LOCOMOTION
United Kingdom

THE LOCOMOTION
Japan

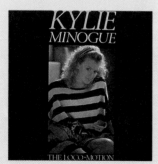

THE LOCOMOTION
Scandinavia

JE NE SAIS PAS POURQUOI
Australia

IT'S NO SECRET
U.S.A.

ESPECIALLY FOR YOU
The world

HAND ON YOUR HEART
United Kingdom

KYLIE VIDEOS

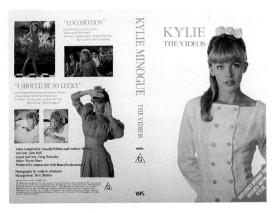

KYLIE – THE VIDEOS
Australia and New Zealand only

KYLIE MINOGUE – THE VIDEOS
Rest of the world

THE KYLIE COLLECTION
Australia and New Zealand only

THE KYLIE MINOGUE
FAN CLUB

The addresses to write to are:

Australia and New Zealand
Private Bag 5, Albert Park 3206, Melbourne, Australia
Rest of the World
P.O. Box 292, Watford, Hertfordshire, England WD2 4ND

WRITTEN BY: Chrissie Camp
DESIGNED BY: Gerard Brennan, Cactus Design
PHOTOGRAPHERS: Grant Matthews, Peter Mac, Andrew Lehman, Bill Bachman,
Andy Tavares & Kylie Minogue
Neighbours photographs courtesy Channel 10, Melbourne
MANAGEMENT: Terry Blamey